BLOCKCHAIN REVOLUTION

UNDERSTANDING THE INTERNET OF MONEY

BY SMART READS

Free Audiobook

As a thank you for being a Smart Reader you can choose 2 FREE audiobooks from audible.com. Simply sign up for free by visiting www.audibletrial.com/Travis to get your books.

Visit:
www.smartreads.co/freebooks
to receive Smart Reads books for FREE

Check us out on Instagram:
www.instagram.com/smart_readers
@smart_readers

ABOUT SMARTREADS

Choose Smart Reads and get smart every time. Smart Reads sorts through all the best content and condenses the most helpful information into easily digestible chunks.

We design our books to be short, easy to read and highly informative. Leaving you with maximum understanding in the least amount of time.

Smart Reads aims to accelerate the spread of quality information so we've taken the copyright off everything we publish and donate our material directly to the public domain. You can read our uncopyright below.

We believe in paying it forward and donate 5% of our net sales to Pencils of Promise to build schools, train teachers and support child education.

To limit our footprint and restore forests around the globe we are planting a tree for every 10 hardcover books we sell.

Thanks for choosing Smart Reads and helping us help the planet.

Sincerely,

Travis & the Smart Reads Team

Uncopyright 2017 by Smart Reads. No rights reserved worldwide. Any part of this publication may be reproduced or transmitted in any form without the prior written consent of the publisher.

Disclaimer: The publisher and author make no representations or warranties with respect to the accuracy or completeness of these contents and disclaim all warranties for a particular purpose. The author or publisher is not responsible for how you use this information. The fact that an individual or organization is referred to in this document as a citation or source of information does not imply that the author or publisher endorses the information that the individual or organization provided.

.

TABLE OF CONTENTS

Introduction	2
Chapter 1: The Functionality of Blockchain	9
Chapter 2: Reasons Not To Use Blockchain	15
Chapter 3: Mistakes To Avoid When Using Blockchain	27
Chapter 4: Is The Blockchain The Best Thing For You?	29
Chapter 5: What Can A Blockchain Be Used For?	38
Chapter 6: It's In Your Power To Take Advantage	42
Conclusion	47
Smart Reads Vision	55

INTRODUCTION

Where blockchain can lead us to, and how useful it can be, is not *totally* clear just yet. It's still early days. But what is clear is that the people that matter in the tech and finance worlds are already getting a slice of the Blockchain pie. Already, they can see potential for big things. Even huge world banks such as Santander and Deutsche Bank are getting on board. Why? Because they can see how Blockchain can help make payments quicker and more transparent.

If they can see all this, you need to start seeing it, too. There is no doubt that a blockchain explosion is on its way. You might not be able to see it clearly at the moment, but you should certainly be able to feel the auditory vibrations. Like an army marching to war, it's coming - and it's getting louder. The blockchain boom is shaping up. You don't want to miss out or be late to the party. Remember, just like you're thinking of getting on board with blockchain, so are your rivals.

This book is a great place to start your journey.

Why This Book?

In this book, you will learn about both the brief history of this new concept, as well as what you can do with it.

I will also ground you in the factors, which make it unique, as well as the arguments made against it - and why these arguments are wrong. The biggest takeaway you'll get from this book is the knowledge of whether or not blockchain is what you need and can use right now, and - if it is - how you can use it to your advantage.

At the moment, you might still be a bit confused as to what blockchain tech is. Perhaps you only recently heard about it, found out that money can be made out of it, and decided to see for yourself what it's all about.

Even though Blockchain has been around for almost a decade, there is still confusion as to what it is. People especially find it difficult to describe it to someone. For example, some people refer to it as a crypto-currency (which is essentially what it is), while others use it to refer to bitcoin's infrastructure. Some even swap it for the "smart contracts," as it essentially means the same thing.

Others say it's nothing more than a spreadsheet that can be accessed by everyone around the world, and this is essentially what it is.
But although the usage and definition varies according to each individual, what we can be sure of is the initial function of a blockchain, which is to store a number of

transactions in a decentralized way - as opposed to the way a bank traditionally stores your transactions centrally.

We can also understand it as **Bitcoin's key innovation,** a tool that could potentially be used for cloud computing, online voting and even land registries (more on all this later.)

Blockchain In A Complex Nutshell
To help you understand what Blockchain is, you could try thinking of it like Lego. You can use Lego to make a number of things, but whatever you make will share similarities with everything else you make using Lego, despite how different they may look at first sight.

We use blockchain for data storage and most of the data is financial. Every single block holds a certain transaction's data, and each time a change is made in the chain, the change is replicated automatically across the whole network.

As well as holding certain information, each block also holds a time stamp. The way it uses a network is interesting, as it does without a central server. This is unusual. Instead, the process is decentralized and spread out to include anyone with access to the blockchain. This means a blockchain could potentially be spread to thousands and thousands of data nodes, which use an advanced system to communicate.

There are a variety of users with access to Blockchain's. There are those who can read info but cannot add any new blocks, while there are those who can both read info and add new blocks.

Blockchain's are vulnerable to attack from hackers just like any data is, but they are in general very safe. This is thanks to the formidable computational power that is needed to adjust a chain's validity. As such, it makes little sense for a hacker to spend time trying to hack a blockchain.

Simple Roots Made Simple
Some people say that blockchain is the most important thing to have been invented since the Internet. It made its first appearance in 2008, when P2P wanted to do without banks when it came to making transactions. The ideas that people came up with were outlined in a text titled *Bitcoin: A P2P Electronic Cash System*.

Not long afterwards, the first blockchain code was relaxed as a concept. A number of developers heard about it and got on board.

Understanding Bitcoin is essential to understanding

Blockchain. An increasingly popular electronic currency that is starting to rival PayPal, Bitcoin allows its users to transfer whole Bitcoin's or parts of a Bitcoin with other users in order to pay for services and goods. The receiver of the Bitcoin can then sell it on for hard currency or do a trade with someone else.

Blockchain tracks and records each individual transaction publicly, so anyone can download and take a look at them. The transaction is checked one by one to confirm authenticity and whoever verifies the transaction receives a fragment of a bitcoin. This is a process called mining for bitcoins and is essentially what keeps the decentralized network running.

Each bitcoin is valued according to the amount of bit coins that are in circulation, as well as current exchange rates. Prices also fluctuate according to supply and demand in much the same way that traditional currencies do.

Five years after its creation, the blockchain started to take off and 2014 was seen as a watershed year for blockchain. It was at this time when individuals were able to use their knowledge to slot while programs into blocks, and also non-financial data, too. As such, it is not possible to use block chains to conduct complex statements centered on the transfer of funds. In 2016,

Russia's government deliberated over whether their financial problems could be solved with blockchain.

Why Blockchain And Not A Conventional Database?
Good question. Perhaps the biggest difference between a conventional database and the blockchain is the amount of centralization. In a conventional database, data nodes and servers are often separated to cater for the limitations of physical space. This is decentralization, but on a minimal scale. Moreover, efforts are made so that the data and servers are as close as can be. Latency is unwanted!

The nodes found in blockchain databases, however, are spread out across the world - they can literally be anywhere! This means that if there is a glitch and something goes wrong with a node in Peru, the network can still function. Amazing. What this means is that info in any blockchain has answers to no single master or country, which makes the information super egalitarian. The fact that the blockchain can also scan for tampering, as well as sort itself, means it's totally safe and autonomous. There are always checks and balances so that risk is decreased.
As you can probably imagine, the way currency transactions are handled has now changed irrevocably. Blockchain tech is a game changer. Just like the Internet paved the way for information to be

swapped digitally, Bitcoin has paved the way for currency to be transferred digitally.

CHAPTER 1: THE FUNCTIONALITY OF BLOCKCHAIN

It is the cryptography that protects the Blockchain and makes it so useful. Literally *anyone* can view a blockchain without worrying that they're going to compromise its security. Why is the security so good? Primarily because it's decentralized.

Basically, when a block is added to a blockchain, it features every last bit of data from the last transaction - as well as all the transactions before that one. Before a block is added to a chain, each of its nodes and data is checked and confirmed by looking at all the preceding transactions. As such, it's practically impossible to develop a fake transmission. Just think for a second how much fake info would need to be generated in order to fool the system. It hardly seems worth it.

Info Transmission
A blockchain's info is usually separated into 2 types:

- Transactions
- Blocks

A lot of the info in block chains feature numerous transactions in which individuals have - and are continuing - to move finance data here and there. Once a transaction is successfully completed, the info passes through a database intact, as a single unit, replying on a model that helps it to find nodes quickly so that it can jump from place to place seamlessly. It doesn't need to rely on any one of us to guide it - everything is done automatically.

A transaction becomes valid when it is digitally verified and signed. It can't be valid before then because of the possibility of replica transactions. Furthermore, every single block is filled with data that helps the whole chain to confirm each transaction, as well as its own unique place in the block chain. Once a transaction has been verified, miners, who are compensated in bitcoin, make new blocks.

Accessibility
A block chain *can* be viewed by all and sundry, but it is up to the creator to decide this. They may want to set it to private instead. If a block chain is public, it means that anyone who accesses it is doing so with standard safeguards that have already been set in place. This protects everyone from corruption or hacking.

As you can imagine, public block chains are harder to create and control. Consequently, they have bigger costs. For this reason, users are incentivized to verify transactions by the lure of bitcoin. Blockchain's that are private are much cheaper because they can only be accessed by a select (and usually small) amount of people.

In a bitcoin network, anyone who downloads a Bitcoin Core agrees to run bitcoin nodes while also agreeing to verify a few transactions, too. As such, new blocks are generated and attached to a chain. These will then await verification. If blockchain's are set to private, only people who have the right clearance can verify transactions.

Being Careful
Any transaction entering a node will be copied automatically into the node's chain. But before it is accepted, all preceding transactions must be verified first. There is thus no need for external data management because all the individual nodes have an inherent understanding of what they should do with any new block.

Also, any new block is able to create an original proof of work system that relies on powerful computation in order to work. Because the computational system is so powerful, crypto currencies are largely safe from attack - it would require a hugely expensive system to hack into it.

Harsh Functions

This is a mathematical function that strengthens a block chain's security system. In private chains, harsh functions convert legible data into fixed length output. To use an analogy, this is an info fingerprint. There are various sorts of harsh functions, with the most popular one being the SHA-256.

A harsh function is assigned to all newly created blocks automatically, even if they are not used. Each function is super specific, which means that even if you change just one number the whole of the harsh function is rearranged in such a variety of ways that decryption is tricky unless you have the right authorization.

Moreover, extra info is then attached to a harsh function according to where the block is in the chain, as well as what data it is storing. If a block's harsh function tries to pair up with a node that has a different harsh function, the block won't be allowed automatically into the blockchain.

Architecture:

The first advantage that the architecture of a block chain provides is that every node has its own unique talent for generating a group agreement, while simultaneously working independently when carrying out other tasks. The block chain operates in such a way that even if rogue nodes decided to work with ulterior motives, their suspicious content would be spotted, isolated and removed. The only time it might not be spotted and removed is if the attack was big and sophisticated.

Nodes that are finding it difficult to connect to new info will often look to well-connected nodes for advice. To be sure, nodes will always double-check a fresh transaction to make sure the info is 100% accurate before they enter the block. A protocol offers an extra safeguard, spotting and removing conflicting and replica data before a new block is let through.

Other Sorts Of Block Chains
Ledger-based chains are the most popular. The second most popular type of blockchain is a side chain. A side chain - as the name might suggest - is distinct from the original in that, while it is tied to it, it doesn't interact until it has finished its own transactions.

Another type of chain is the alt-chain (alternative chain). These add a bit more service to what could otherwise be a fairly limited chain format. They look to correct a few problems, including increasing storage, adding anonymity, as well as boosting overall performance. Alt-chains are often used together with what we refer to as smart contracts, and they are programmed to activate as soon as a certain set of commands have been acted upon. Essentially, you can look at an alt-chain as cutting out the middleman.

What Else Can You Use Blockchain For?
Time Stamps:
If you want to track your transactions without using crypto currency, you can use time stamps. Because a blockchain organizes its data with so much structure, it is fairly easy to work out exactly when something happened.

Storage:
More and more companies and apps in the cloud storage sense are catching into Blockchain, exploring how they can use it to perform numerous functions, including monitoring data exchange. They are also taking a close look at how much paying for storage would cost.

Licensing:
Soon, it is hoped that block chains will be used to license and pay for digital items and content. This is still in its early stages, and only a handful of digital content is able to connect to certain bank accounts before deducting a certain amount for each use.

Social Media:
The big guns of social media are exploring ways of generating chains which individuals are connected to, so that they can get hold of a digital account for their whole history. Eventually, it is reckoned that all your experiences and achievements will be "digitally imprinted."

Public Systems:
A public system, as its name might suggest, can be interacted with by anyone whenever they want. Ethereum and Bitcoin are just two chains that have no centralized body determining their growth. Because there are still checks and balances, the whole chain will also go smoothly and accurately. You play by the rules automatically once you sign up.

Private Systems:
Private systems are also not subject to central authority per say, but there is a governing body if we take individuals who have been granted to interact and verify the transactions as a government body. A private chain may not be being used for conventional data, but it still has its uses in that it creates numerous backups and fail safes of critical data automatically, while at the same time tightening up a system's resilience to faults.

CHAPTER 2: REASONS NOT TO USE BLOCKCHAIN

Like many new things in life, Blockchain has its critics. In this chapter, we'll explore the most common criticisms of Blockchain.

Rise In Costs
Blockchain's have its advantages, but being inexpensive to run isn't one of them. Weirdly enough, the fact that Blockchain is so inefficient is actually what makes it as secure as it is! But you have to look at it like this way. Each node that is created will cost what it consumes in resources, and every single node is pretty much going to cost the same. You won't get a node that is dirt cheap.

As such, the blockchain can be seen as largely cost-prohibitive, which can often put people off from using it. This is particularly true when an individual decides that they don't really need to use a blockchain. It can be seen as something of an expensive luxury that many can afford to overlook.

Every single confirmed bitcoin transaction costs roughly as much as it costs you to power your home for roughly a day and a half. That's already a lot of money, but the cost is going to keep going up as the node system continues to expand.

Scant Data Monitoring
We live in a world where targeted ads are everywhere. In this world, the more info a company can get about you as a consumer, the better. This means that the blockchain, by virtue of it being encrypted, is actually bad news for advertisers. Why? Because they won't be able to get the info they need about you in order to target you with the right ads! To enter the mainstream, blockchain needs aggregation and recommendation tech to be re-evaluated.

It's Complicated
The blockchain means that anyone who owns a smartphone and has a bitcoin account can theoretically run a small Internet company. However, blockchain could scupper their plans because it's so complex. You might be asking, "But what about basic block chains? Aren't *they* super simple?" No, they're not. Even the basic ones are complicated! If blockchain is going to enter the mainstream, it HAS to be a lot simpler. It needs to be streamlined.

It Can Be Tampered With
Despite being cost prohibitive, Blockchain is still vulnerable to attacks from hackers and hijackers. Hijacking a chain is easy enough for anyone with the

know-how and motivation. As such, if blockchain does go mainstream, it would need someone to come along and make it tamper proof. You can do this by using a huge amount of computational resources so that a large amount of blocks are crammed with changed info. When verifying info, the lengthier chains have more authority over shorter ones, with the result being that they have precedence.

Basically, what I mean by this is that an invading party could flood a chain once a transaction has been made and therefore use the exact same finances many times over and over again. So what happens is that a product gets sent, yet the funds have not progressed any further from where they were at the beginning. At the moment, this isn't really worth such a cost, thanks to the fact that there are many options when it comes to making a transaction with bitcoin. But if we want blockchain to enter the mainstream, such a glaring loophole needs to be taken cared of.

Established Companies Will Benefit The Most:
As mentioned, blockchain does cost a fair amount of money. As such, it's only really beneficial at the moment to businesses who already have good infrastructure, and who can afford to spend money on blockchain while enjoying its benefits.

Saying that blockchain is something which can be used by everyone (both small and large businesses alike) is misleading at best, and totally untrue at worst. At the moment, small businesses can't really afford to take a gamble on it.

Blockchain Can Actually Give Rise To New Security Issues:
It's possible to lower the risk of potential threats from hackers and this is in the hands of those who are verifying the transactions. However, it depends WHO is verifying the transactions. It's impossible to examine everyone's profile, and those who verify the transactions are largely anonymous. We have to trust that they are working ethically, but the fact of the matter is that should they wish to take advantage of the system, they can do so fairly easily. If we want blockchain to go mainstream, we need to implement more checks and balances.

Trading Will Stay The Same:
If you want to grasp what exactly blockchain does for asset trading, you need to know that there is a difference between settlements and *gross* settlements that occur on the same day. The best ones for the buyer are same-day settlements because shares are handed out quickly if you're working with blockchain. Ordinarily, you would be kept waiting for around

three days. Blockchain accelerates the process and will keep on doing so as and when (or if) it enters the mainstream.

Yes, same day settlements are nothing new. But you can't get them in all exchanges. Saudi Arabia has been offering them for some time, but traditional habits and ways of regulating things are still largely the way of things in most countries.

Gross settlements of the realtime kind are not an especially attractive idea, particularly for any pro traders that like to net at the time of making a trading decision. Let's look at it like this: say that you're heading out to a restaurant for dinner with a friend. You've left your wallet at home, so your friend offers to pay for all the food. You two go out again and this time you pay for everything. As far as you're concerned, the two of you are even, if the cost of the meals weren't the same. This happens in a stock market arena, where pro traders settle at the end of each day, rather than settling every time they make a transaction.

Blockchain Can't Spread So Fast - If It Does, It Won't Improve:
We want blockchain to reach the mainstream - but not too soon. And right now, it's too soon. It's got a lot of good things going for it, but it also has a few kinks that

we need to iron out first. So, we need to strike a balance: we want blockchain to grow its user base so that it can keep developing, but if too many people adopt it too quickly, the necessary improvements just won't get made.

Ideally, what we want is growth that is slow but also steady. Yes, it will take longer to reach our goals than people might like, but the end-results will be worth it.

Unfortunately, as much as I've stated that decentralization is good for blockchain, it's bad in the sense that centralization can at least instigate positive growth and take something forward thanks to a unified goal. Without centralization, there is no one specific growth or idea about which direction blockchain should head in.

The Internet faced a similar scenario in its early stages. It needed someone to concentrate on the issue of TCP/IP and cover the costs - unfortunately; there was no such individual around. Over time, the issue was eradicated, but without a leading authority figure, the issue took longer to eliminate than it could have.

CHAPTER 3: MISTAKES TO AVOID WHEN YOU USING BLOCKCHAIN

I've seen lots of people jump onto the Blockchain bandwagon without thinking things through properly. They see all the hype around it, get excited and dive straight into things without much thought. However, before you begin, it's worth asking **why** you are implementing a Blockchain and **what** exactly you want to do with it.

Once you have answered both these questions, you then need to avoid the other popular mistakes people make when implementing a Blockchain. To help you out, I'm going to use this chapter to highlight exactly what these errors are.

Your Expectations Are Unrealistic
There is a lot of hype around Blockchain at the moment. It reminds me of the hype that surrounded the Internet when it first became mainstream. And the problem with hype is that it builds unrealistic expectations in our heads. We expect a LOT more from something when it comes "hyped-up." And that's exactly what's happening with blockchain at the moment.

A blockchain is a database. Is it better than your

average database? Not really. It can't solve all your problems, and it can't really perform any more functions than a conventional database. And yet it costs more money. So, first of all, ask yourself, why you are using blockchain and not any other type of database? If it's because blockchain is going to change your world, you're using it for the wrong reasons.

Also, block chains can't store masses and masses of info, any more than a regular database can. Look, you don't want to bloat a node with info. If you do, that node will then bloat all subsequent nodes all along the chain.

Look at it like this, a whole bitcoin blockchain can hold around 55 GB of info. As you can see, even the most efficient block chains don't store masses of data. They have no need to.

Also, yes, a blockchain has plenty of safeguards ready so that it can mitigate the impact of incomplete or duplicate blocks. But this doesn't mean that it is entirely invulnerable to user mistakes. Even expert employees can be left perplexed if a block in the chain can only be identified by a complex hash key. Operating your blockchain is NOT as simple as sitting at your desk and working on an active node.

Rushing Into Things

Lots of people get a bit giddy when they first hear about blockchain, especially if they're coming from Reddit. They want to dive straight into it without fully understanding all the intricacies. Doing this will just set you up for a huge fall.

If you want to start and end a blockchain properly, you need to take some time to fully understand it. This is imperative. And when I say time, I mean a fair amount of time. This isn't something you can pick up in a few minutes.

This book is a good place to start, but it's really only that - a starting point. You will need to continue your research once this book is finished if you want to get the most out of blockchain. If you don't, your blockchain will not be able to serve the purposes you have in mind.

First of all, ask yourself what you want to use a blockchain for. Only once you have a clear answer can you then find a piece of creation software which is going to take you forward without slowing you down or setting you back. There are many to choose from. Unlike the blockchain, creation software is already mainstream and the market is crammed with different ones.

I can't overstate at this point how important it is that you take your time choosing the right software. Making the wrong choice really can set you back big time. Do proper research and don't rush into choosing the first one you see.

Lack Of Patience
Once you have a clear understanding of what you'll be using Blockchain for, it's still important that you don't rush things. Instead, you should continue to work at a deliberate pace so you don't make any mistakes.

It can take a while to set up a blockchain, and the process can be complex and more difficult than people assume. But it's key that you don't try to cut corners, and that you instead do everything by the book as it were. If you rush during the setup procedure, you might find there are lots of mistakes to iron out later on. And this will take up time and cause you a great degree of hassle.

I suggest drawing up a timetable or schedule before you make a start so that you always know what you need to do, when you need to do it and how long you expect it to take. As long as you take your time and follow my suggestions, there is no reason why implementing your own blockchain won't go smoothly. It should go from an idea to a reality without any issues.

No Limited Access
Blockchain is an exciting piece of new tech and as such lots of people want to give it a go. I recommend keeping your blockchain private and only letting people who have had proper training access it. If you let an inexperienced individual into your chain, it could derail what you've got. Inaccurate info can easily clip the wings of a fledgling chain.

Also, if you do decide to go private, you should store your info in a secure location so that if you do lose it, there is no way that a scrupulous individual could access it and take control of your chain.

Failing To Understand The Differences Between Regular and Smart Contracts
Regular contracts and smart contracts are two different things - with more differences than commonalities. But because the blockchain is still so new, it's easy for wrong info to travel far and wide without anything to counter it quickly enough.

Smart contracts differ from regular contracts in that they aren't a legally binding document or agreement. They're more of a process that is automated and triggered whenever specific factors occur. For example, let's say you used a smart contract to pay off your car on the monthly until it's fully paid off. Because you have used a smart contract, you are not legally bound to meet the monthly payment. It's rather arbitrary.

Smart contracts *can* be used as a **part** of any legally binding document/agreement. As an example, let's say you've signed a legally binding contract that states you have to meet certain monthly repayments. As part of this contract, a smart contract may have been used as a clause, so if you default on a monthly payment, your car's battery is cut so that you cannot use it.

Smart contracts also differ to Ricardian contracts, which determine liability legally. Smart contracts are activated only after numerous episodes of liability, and even then nobody is under any obligation to act. A smart contract is activated or it isn't. There isn't any in-between.

Smart contracts can also be programmed in such a way that they perform certain functions and look out for various variables. However, they are strictly a binary process that triggers certain outcomes. External events control them, which ultimately restricts what they can and cannot do. It's worth

mentioning, though, that there aren't as many restrictions as there used to be, and there will be even less in the future. As such, there are more things that smart contracts can be used for.
Eventually, more and more people will start using blockchain, and as they do, the technology will get better, and we will be able to use it for more things. You might think there are a finite number of functions at the moment - and it's true, the number of functions are limited - but the various *uses* for these functions is astonishing. As long as you have a set of transactions and a Wi-Fi connection, all routine actions with clear factors in terms of failure of success can be used by a smart contract and blockchain.

Before I end this chapter, I want to say that, while a smart contract generally takes over a single block in the chain, both are separate entities. They might be used in conjunction every now and then, but they are still different. Try to keep them apart in your head. I know this can be tricky, which is why you should look at it like this:

- Blockchain - Holds all info, distributed database
- Smart contract - Activates remaining info when needed, distributed computing

CHAPTER 4: IS THE BLOCKCHAIN THE BEST THING FOR YOU?

If at this point in time you feel as though the blockchain is best suited to your needs, you will still need to carry out a bit of experimentation to see what works and what doesn't. Moreover, you still can't be sure whether this is going to be the right thing for you.

For example, some users soon realize that blockchain is too complicated for them.

If you experiment, you get a better feel for the blockchain. You'll find out how easy or difficult it is to use and implement. It's like with anything in life - you should always try before you buy.

Reading Data
It's fairly easy to see which individuals are accessing what on a traditional database. This information is usually stored in a set of log files. The blockchain, however, requires you to access it via a database node. As soon as any changes have been made to the chain or a block, the alterations are recorded in a conventional log file. Any files that need securing, the blockchain is a solid solution - especially if these same files need to be accessed by people who are allowed to look, but who aren't allowed to touch.

Write Data

Conventional databases are usually secured by a password and username, though there are also other additional means of authentication to make something extra secure. Digital signatures in addition to the security I have already touched upon protect block chains. This additional security is activated whenever you add new data or a transaction to a chain. This helps to make it easier to track each transaction (who made it and where it came from).

Each time an individual completes a transaction, all participants must sign it digitally to confirm it. This step can be skipped if you add info to the node instead. But each time another block is attached, a separate signature is needed by whoever the verifier is. Until it is added, the block cannot be attached to the blockchain.

There will be circumstances when direct ID isn't needed, but even in these cases the IP address of those who are interacting with the chain is recorded.

Altering Data

There may be other storage types that you find more useful, though the amount of storage types depends on how much you'll be changing the data that your chain will be needed for.

In a conventional database with a central authority, anyone who has prestigious authority is able to rewrite and change data using a log that records everything that has been altered. However, this doesn't happen in a blockchain. In such a decentralized system, any altered data is rejected because it doesn't conform to a chain's standards.

If you'd like to alter data in your chain, you need to alter it at the same time across most of the nodes in your database. This takes a lot of time. As secure as the blockchain is, the fact that it is so demanding means that many users are continuing to avoid it when choosing their database.

Backing Up Data:
Conventional databases wait for user authorization before updating. Blockchain, however, updates its nodes automatically each time a user adds a block to the chain. For this reason, they are a solid choice if you have hugely valuable information. Basically, it's very unlikely that the majority of the nodes will fail at the same time so that your data is put at risk.

Data That Is Decentralized:
The distance that exists between two nodes isn't usually relevant, but when you need to access a fair

amount of nodes frequently, or whenever you need specific info, the blockchain is limited in that it doesn't have the exact answer the way it is at the moment. This should not automatically rule out blockchain as a storage solution, but you will need to add extra precautionary measures while noting the location of all your nodes.

Interoperability:
If you want to use an internal chain, you can connect the chain to other ones used by separate individuals and groups easily and for a certain specified period of time. You do this if you want other people to access your database, and it is this feature among others that distinguishes the blockchain apart from regular databases.

It goes without saying that you need to be careful about who gets access to your chain. Do checks on them first because they will be able to access *everything*.

Volume Of Data:
One of the things you should take into consideration when deciding whether or not the blockchain is the right database for you if the amount of info you will putting into the individual blocks.

Tip - you don't want this data to be large or complex. Why? Because transferring big, complex files over large distances between the individual nodes takes up more time than you might imagine. I promise you. If you're to be working with hefty, complex files, it's a much better idea to use a conventional database that will let you work with data with a lot less stress and hassle. Moreover, databases with a central authority are also much better suited to write speed.

Costs of Validation:
Want to know how much validation for running your chain will cost you? To work this out, you need to first of all identify the type/sort of data that will make up the individual blocks.

Remember this: The blocks with the least amount of data cost the least to validate. It's basic math. The more data you put into a block, the more money it will set you back. You might think that you could spread the data around a lot of blocks. For example, you have a lot of data but by putting just a small amount in several blocks, as opposed to a huge chunk in one or two blocks, you might assume you will save money. You won't.

Validation is tricky, which is why I suggest that you either ask someone with experience to do it, or you pay someone to do it. Give them an incentive. This works especially well in private systems, where users need to first sign a contract beforehand whereby they agree to abide by your rules.

If your chain proves to be popular, things can get ever more costlier. When this happens, you can offset the costs with a series of incentives. Every single validator incurs more costs, but look at it like this: Every single validator also means more security, which protects your whole system. Every time a transaction is verified, your system will become less prone to errors. It's a win-win situation.

What Happens Next?
If you've decided that, yes, the blockchain is for you, the next step you take depends on what you want to use your chain for. If you own a business and want to get onboard with the blockchain trend, your next step will be to see how you can use block chains and smart contracts to enhance the ancillary side of your company, particularly in terms of growing revenue, reducing costs and overall boosting efficiency while keeping on the good side of both shareholders and customers.

You will also need to examine the various ways the blockchain is able to help you stand out from your rivals, giving you a competitive edge by moving you forward. Ideally, you want to catch a trend before your rivals. Nobody wants to be the second or third Facebook - we want to be the first.

Also, now is the time to think about the ways in which blockchain might affect the status quo - and what you can do to protect your business from being harmed by this too much. Blockchain could be a game changer, and you don't want it to catch you by surprise. Remember - if you know what's around the corner, you can be ready for it. Get onboard with the blockchain before it blows past your window like a tornado, leaving your business in pieces.

Your reasons for using the blockchain may be different. For example, perhaps you want to enter the mainstream from another entrance and your plan is for the chain to act as your path that gets you there. If this sounds like something you want to do, you need to experiment with public block chains as soon as you can and as much as you can. Dedicate some time getting to know them and growing them because if you want the blockchain to enter the mainstream in order to complete your own goals, just know it can't do that without your help.

If an open network works better and experiences few

issues, the public will obviously use them to solve problems. This is where your business comes in. Always begin with a clear a goal when it comes to solving a problem, before planning how many ways you can use blockchain to solve the said problem. Every time you come up with a new solution, the process becomes more streamlined. As such, the public will pay attention more and more as you reveal the chain and its effectiveness to the world.

If you aren't sure what your plans are just yet, no problem. However, you will need to decide at some point. My advice is you turn to outside sources for help. Ask people who are using blockchain. Visit forums, do research. Find out what people are doing with it.

The future of this type of database is still misty, but one thing is for sure: It's not a fad or a gimmick. It's already been around for almost a decade and it isn't going away. As such, there will come a time when it enters the mainstream. At which point, your rivals will have already perfected it. Don't be late to the party. Irrespective of your plans, as much as there will be innovations to the blockchain, there will also be constants. Moreover, lots of people and businesses will get on board with it, and many will fail. Some will get to the top, but only after a period of struggle. There will be old faces competing alongside new ones, with the new ones striving to do everything in a new way. In short, not everyone wins at blockchain. There will be losers. Don't let yourself be one of them.

CHAPTER 5: WHAT CAN BLOCKCHAIN BE USED FOR?

Still unsure about whether or not the Blockchain is right for you? Or maybe you think it is - but aren't sure about what it could be used for.

When something new comes out that we're unsure about, we have a tendency to look around us and see what others are doing with it. They lead and we follow. The potential use for Blockchain is massive. But right now, you're likely at a loss on what it can be used for.

The truth is that Blockchain can be applied to many forms of agreement, contracts, register or record keeping that the possibilities are vast and almost limitless. World governments are starting to sniff around it, wondering what in the heck they could use it for. Public services anyone? In this chapter, I'm going to explore the things Blockchain can be used for (apart from Bitcoin, of course).

Digital Identities
Digital security is a big worry for many of us, myself included. But especially for those who have a lot to protect, digital security is a constant worry. But imagine if you could remove that problem?

Digital security IS a big worry. It costs the industry around $18,500,000,000 a year, which means that for every $ spent, a dollar is going on ad fraud. Blockchain makes it easier to track and manage our digital identity. It also makes tracking them more efficient and secure. This means less fraud and easy sign-ons.

Authorization is, after all, deeply ingrained in culture and commerce all over the world. Be it healthcare, banking national security, online retailing and citizenship documentation, it's everywhere. Let's take what happened to Target as an example.

At retailing giant Target, a data breach was reported that, as it turned out, was much bigger and broader than everyone assumed. A whopping **70,000,000** customers' key info (address, name, phone number etc.) was hacked. This is the paradox of a technologically advanced society: We want to advance in such a way that all our info is stored on a database so that everything is made easier (such as buying and selling goods, as well as marketing), but it comes with a huge security risk. Breached accounts and hacked databases happen.

Blockchain is a solid solution to problems with digital identity. With the blockchain, identity is uniquely authenticated in a secure, immutable and totally irrefutable way. At the moment, we are reliant on methods, which store passwords and "secret answers" on insecure systems. The blockchain method, by contrast, is an authentication system that is based on immutable ID verification with digital signatures that are based on public-key cryptography.

Distributed Cloud Storage
In the future, blockchain data storage will be a huge disruptor. Why? At the moment, cloud store services all have a central authority. All users have to put all their trust in one storage provider who essentially controls each and every one of your online assets. With Blockchain, everything is decentralized. More and more businesses are realizing the importance of this and are already beta-testing with Blockchain.

And if you have more storage capacity than you need, in a blockchain-powered network you can actually rent it out so that it doesn't go to waste. If I were a business such as Uber or Airbnb, I would be taking a very close look at distributed cloud storage solutions.

Trading
Yes, Blockchain can be used in the world of trading. Bitcoin's are now being traded, with the logical result that Blockchain networks are starting to be used more

and more. Nasdaq has already begun using Blockchain in what is one of the world's biggest private stock markets.

Decentralized Notary

A really interesting feature of Blockchain is time stamp. A whole blockchain network validates a state of hash (or piece of data), at specific, certain times. Because it is decentralized, it can affirm the existence of a transaction (or whatever) that can be further proven in a court of law. Up until this point, it was centralized notary services alone that could do this.

There are really no limits with Blockchain when it comes to data and record keeping. Whatever profession or industry you're involved in, it will be of infinite use to you.

CHAPTER 6: IT'S IN YOUR POWER TO TAKE ADVANTAGE

If you do decide to use blockchain in order to develop your smart contracts, you will then need to download Ethereum, a design space which works well with the blockchain. The currency is called ether, which finances labor transactions between people. You can also use it to host or use applications on the Ethereum site. At the moment, a single ether equates to just over $12.

What Is Ethereum?
It's essentially a distributed database, which can host applications (decentralized ones) which all work like any individual node like one of your chains would. The apps can provide you with a direct route of accessing your created smart contracts, meaning they are able to receive and send data from any conventional node (decentralized) that is within close proximity to where you are. You don't *have* to run an Ethereum node through the conventional node, but my advice is that you give it a go as doing so will make it much easier for you to test your smart contracts.

If your plan is to do the programming yourself, you would be well advised to use a programming language called **Solidity**, which is related to JavaScript. It employs a .sol or a.s extension, as well as LLL. If you have already tried your hand at Python or Serpent, using **Solidity** should be easy enough. If you're not sure about trying it, let me tell you that it's now outdoing both Python and Serpent in terms of popularity.

When you create contracts, you will need to compile them. To do this, I suggest using C++ solc Compiler. Maybe you won't like it - if not, you could try Cosmo.

Once the contracts have been compiled, you will then need to turn your attention to Ethereum Web3.ja API. Without this, it will be impossible for JavaScript to work, as it lets you interact directly with your contracts without the need of logging into each node (which is a lot of hassle).

Frameworks
You will notice a lot of frameworks have already been created by developers, all (or at least most) of which are available for free. Why are they free? Because these developers want this market to grow as much as possible. Charging fees for the frameworks would only stunt growth. I definitely recommend that you use an existing framework because building your own is a.) time consuming and b.) tricky.

Embark and Truffle

I like Truffle because it automates most of the typical programming processes. This means you have more time to concentrate on coming up with some top code before testing, compiling and deploying any alterations that need to be made as fast and as hassle-free as possible. Embark, meanwhile, comes in handy when you need to streamline your testing and building process.

Meteor

When working on this part of the process, most people go with Meteor. It comes with web3.js, and is also a general web app framework. Again, this is one of those stacks that you might be unsure of or resistant to. But I suggest that you start learning it now, because it WILL grow in popularity. And wouldn't you rather be ahead of your rivals, as opposed to trailing behind them?

APIs:

APIs are important, but the most popular one for decentralized apps is BlockApps.net. Why? Because BlockApps.net replicates an Ethereum node whenever you can't produce a node by yourself.

If you don't fancy BlocApps.net, the second most popular is MetaMask. I like this, as it lets you run a standard platform of Ethereum tools, no matter which web browser you're using. LightWallet is another option that you might want to consider. It's good for interacting with apps that have no central authority, but it is rather in-depth. It's really one for the pros.

Let's Build

Okay, so that's all out of the way. Now it's time to build! Before you do anything else, you need to produce an Ethereum node. I use Geth to do this, as it's really easy and is actually the prime interface of all Ethereum nodes.

To get started with Geth, go to your command line before entering bash <(curlhttp://install-geth.ethereum.org. Then, you will see a prompt, which tells you to begin the installation process. To begin, you have to select the right version of Ethereum CLL, as well as your operating system.

The installation will finish, at which point you can start using Geth. You will notice that the environment looks a bit like a console mixed with JavaScript. The console is handy, as it lets you track both your dismal failures and your glorious successes! Now you need to properly start working. Find a terminal tool and open it, before accessing your Geth console. A program will launch and you should see an indicator that is symbolized as > on your screen. This tells you that everything is working smoothly. Whenever you want to quit, just type in "exit" before pressing ENTER. You can use *gethconsole2>>geth.log* as your command whenever you want to redirect or log console output. Once your smart contract is written up with Solidity and you are happy with it, you need to then use solc to compile it.

After the contract is compiled, it's deploying time. You will be charged an ether fee, and there will be a contract to sign with your digital signature. Get this done, and you will receive an address, which is your contracts address in a chain. You will also receive your contacts ABI. With this in your hand, use an API and your smartphone to check it. This *may* cost you more ether.

CONCLUSION: THE FUTURE OF BLOCKCHAIN

It is reckoned that the world of finance could be taken over by Blockchain in the future. That's a big call. But it makes sense that a traceable global currency that is backed up by a strong, efficient and secure infrastructure would cause a huge cost reduction for all those who are participating - and it will cause a huge change in world banking.

Essentially, blockchain can do for **payments** what email previously did for **communication**.

So what's going to change?
Soon, all the central banks will adopt Blockchain. In addition to this, we will start to see cryptographically secure currencies in wider use. Nasdaq has already implemented Blockchain in one of its stock markets and will launch digital technology that is backed by Blockchain, which will enhance the equity management capabilities offered by the Nasdaq Private Market platform.

A settlement of equity, fixed income trades and currency will become pretty much instant via permission distributed ledgers and this will create a key opportunity for banks to enhance efficiency while creating ever new asset classes.

Control

Blockchain has massive potential to lower cyber security risks by using a visible ledger to offer ID authentication. An electronic ledger system will be able to meet the requirements for maintaining, indexing and numbering communication info while recording them.

Car rental agencies will be able to take advantage of Blockchain. For example, they can use smart contracts to allow a rental automatically as soon as insurance info is confirmed and payment is received through the blockchain. And think about refrigerators too. Fixed with sensors and hooked up to the Internet, the fridge can use a blockchain network to control automated interactions with the outside world - such as paying for food and tracking its own warranty! Think of all the hassle it takes away from you having to do these things.

Small businesses can, of course, use blockchain too. They can, for example, use it to form trusted trading platforms with other businesses. The post-trade environment will benefit as well. Blockchain will be able to restore transparency and security to our post-trade world. A bank, meanwhile, can use the Internet to pay its supplier immediately. Moreover, think about timing on risk - Blockchain tech can alter that, too.

And how about crime?
Crime is a big, worrying problem that gives us all a headache. Blockchain is currently being tested by a new startup that hopes to use it to track down and catch criminals faster, more efficiently and cheaper than before.

There may be problems too, of course ...

Banks
Central banks will eventually adopt Blockchain technology and will put cryptographically secure currencies into wide use. Indeed, the blockchain could actually take the place of central banks.

While this wouldn't seem like an entirely bad thing on the surface, there will remain real risks for any bank that decides to work with crypto currency businesses. There is no escaping this fact. However. At the moment, the USB's infrastructure costs are quite high - exorbitant by all accounts. Blockchain tech will (in theory at least) be able to bring down the costs in securities trading, cross-border payments, as well as regulatory compliance by around $20,000,000,000 in just over five years' time.

Also, banks are met with a LOT of applications, both inside and outside. And I mean a LOT. With Blockchain transactions, these applications will be significantly reduced, as the chain's transaction holds all key info for the transfer of contracts and assets. It contains everything that is needed.

At the moment, Deutsche Bank is a bit worried. Their economist has already pointed out that Blockchain is a threat. Why? He says it's because Blockchain lacks the necessary IT infrastructure that would properly support it. And then there is Ethereum, which I have already mentioned. There are many who see it as being more multi-purpose (more of an all-rounder, more *useful*) than Bitcoin. They think it has more potential than Bitcoin and Blockchain - and who knows? They may be right.

However, the world of finance in most of our developed and emerging nations could soon be dominated totally by crypto currencies such as Bitcoin. But if banks are to run a private blockchain, just think about how open it would be to becoming another cartel, the likes of which we have seen many times before. And if that were to happen, it would function just as woefully and as inefficiently as a payments consortium. Not cool. Add to the fact that banks could easily become what we can refer to as the keepers of the cryptographic lock and key.

However, I should also point out that lenders would definitely save money when Blockchain goes mainstream. Indeed, they could save around $20,000,000,000 each year in settlement. That's significant. Lastly, the blockchain tech may even be able to skip our central financial infrastructure altogether.

What does it mean for industries?
Education and time will eventually have a starring role to play. Because right now industries are opening their eyes to the fact that among the Blockchain's core innovations is its adroitness at reducing or totally eradicating trusted counter-parties when it comes to the transaction process.

Blockchain will be helpful to industry, as it can open up new opportunities for business, as well as help them to disrupt processes and technologies that already exist. Blockchain will also be good for globalization, shrinking the world through faster and more efficient transactional activity. Blockchain, in short, will be good for industry.

And what about governments?
The UK government - still reeling from Brexit of course - is just one government that is taking Blockchain very seriously. Already they have taken a

close look at it and are considering what it can do for the public sector.

And indeed, the UK government is not the only government that will be getting onboard with Blockchain. In the future, the way finance is handled in many nations will likely be dominated by crypto currencies such as Bitcoin.

It's been suggested that Blockchain tech could help developing nations distribute their social welfare, improving the living conditions of their subjects faster and more efficiently. In this way, Blockchain could help developing nations to develop much quicker.

Blockchain could also improve the way elections are carried out. At the moment, the election process is often slow and expensive. But by using Blockchain technology, governments can speed them up while reducing the cost.

As you can see, the future of Blockchain is bright. This fresh new technology WILL eventually enter the mainstream, at which point you don't want to be miles behind everyone else. Listen to the hype and get onboard as soon as you can if you are convinced that its uses and advantages will work for YOU.

Thanks for Reading

We really hope you enjoyed this book. If you found this material helpful feel free to share it with friends. You can also help others find it by leaving a review where you purchased the book. Your feedback will help us continue to write books you love.

The Smart Reads library is growing by the day! Make sure and check out the other wonderful books in our catalog. We would love to hear which books are your favorite.

Visit:
www.smartreads.co/freebooks
to receive Smart Reads books for FREE

Check us out on Instagram:
www.instagram.com/smart_readers
@smart_readers

Don't forget your 2 FREE audiobooks.
Use this link www.audibletrial.com/Travis to claim your 2 FREE Books.

SMART READS ORIGINS

Smart Reads was born out of the desire to find the best information fast without having to wade through the sheer volume of fluff available online. Smart Reads combs through massive amounts of knowledge compiles the best into quick to read books on a variety of subjects.

We consider ourselves Smart Readers, not dummies. We know reading is smart. We're self taught. We like to learn a TON about a WIDE variety of topics. We have developed a love for books and we find intelligence attractive.

We found that each new topic we tried to learn about started with the challenge of finding the pieces of the puzzle that mattered most. It can becomes treasure hunt rather than an education.

Smart Reads wants to find the best of the best information for you. To condense it into a package that you can consume in an hour or less. So you can read more books about more topics in less time.

OUR MISSION

Smart Reads aims to accelerate the availability of useful information and will publish a high quality book on every major topic on amazon.

Smart Reads hopes to remove barriers to sharing by taking the copyright off everything we publish and donating it to the public domain. We hope other publishers and authors will follow our example.

Our goal is to donate $1,000,000 or more by 2020 to build over 2,000 schools by giving 5% of our net profit to Pencils of Promise.

We want to Restore forests around the globe by planting a tree for every 10 physical books we sell and hope to plant over 100,000 trees by 2020.

Doesn't it feel good knowing that by educating yourself you are helping the world be a better place!? We think so too...

Thanks for helping us help the world. You Smart Reader you...

Travis and the Smart Reads Team

WHY I STARTED SMART READS

Every time I wanted to learn about something new I'd have to buy 20 books on the topic and spend way too long sorting through them and reading them all until I arrived at the big picture. Until I had enough perspectives to know who was just guessing, who was uninformed and who had stumbled upon something remarkable.

I wished someone else could just go in and figure that out for me and tell me what matters. That's how smart reads was born. I want smart reads to be a company that does all that research up front. Sorts through all the content that is available on each topic and pulls out the most up to date complete understanding, then have people smarter than me package the best wisdom in an easy to understand way in the least amount of words possible.

For example, I got a new puppy so I wanted to learn about dog training. I bought 14 different books about dog training and by the time I got through the first 5 and finally started getting the big picture on the best way to train my puppy she had grown up into a dog.

Yeah she's well behaved. She doesn't poop in the house. I can get her to sit and come when I call. But what if someone else went in and read all those books for me, found the underlying themes and picked out the best information that would give me the big picture and get me right to the point. And I'd only have to read one book instead of 15.

That would be amazing. I would save time. And maybe my dog would be rolling over, cleaning up after my kids and doing the dishes by now. That my friend, is the reason I started smart reads. Because I wanted a company I can trust to deliver me the best information in an easy to understand way that I can digest in under an hour. Because dog training is one of many subjects I want to master.

The quicker I can learn a wide variety of topics the sooner that information can begin playing a role in shaping my future. And none of us knows how long that future will be. So why not do everything we can to make the best of it and consume a ton of knowledge. And I figured all the better if I can also make a positive difference in the world.

That's why we're also building schools, planting trees and challenging ideas about copyright's place in today's world. Because as a company we have to be doing everything we can to support the ecosystem that gives us all these beautiful places to read our books. Thanks for reading.

Travis

Customers Who Bought This Book Also Bought

Success Principles: Techniques for Positive Thinking, Self-Love and Developing a Powerful Mindset

Artificial Intelligence: Understanding A.I. and the Implications of Machine Learning

Understanding Affiliate Marketing: An Internet Marketing Guide for How To Make Money Online Using Products, Websites and Services

Neuro Linguistic Programming: NLP Techniques for Hypnosis, Mind Control, Human Behavior, Relationships, Confidence

Credit Repair Guide: How to Fix Credit Score and Remove Negatives From Credit Report

Self-Esteem Supercharger: Build Self Worth and Find Your Inner Confidence

Develop Self-Discipline: Daily Habit to Make Self Confidence and Will Power Automatic